MY WORDS

by Terrence T. Carter

Ambassador Press, LLC

in the spirit of excellence

Reynoldsburg, OH

Published by Ambassador Press, LLC
PO Box 722 Reynoldsburg, OH 43068
ambpress@insight.rr.com
www.ambassadorpressllc.com

Copyright © 2008 Terrence Carter

Cover Design © 2008 Imagine! Studios™
www.artsimagine.com

All rights reserved. No part of this publication may be reproduced or transmitted in any form or by any means, including informational storage and retrieval systems, without permission in writing from the copyright holder, except for brief quotations in a review.

ISBN 10: 0-9787850-7-X
ISBN 13: 978-0-9787850-7-9

Library of Congress Control Number: 2008943135

First Ambassador Press, LLC printing, December 2008

DEDICATION

I would like to thank all of you who contributed to my first book,

whether it be financially, creative inspiration, or just words of encouragement.

Without these things this would not have been possible.

Terrence T. Carter

TABLE OF CONTENTS

CHAPTER 1: WORDS.....9

Path of Life
Continuing On the Path
The Yesterdays of Me
This is Why I'm Abstinent
Proper Security
My Walk
Surroundings
When My Eyes See Themselves
Why I Write
Writer's Block
Recovery
In the Know
Around You When It's Convenient
Perception
Carpe Diem
Poem for Timyra
The Incoherent Thinking's of Me
Words

CHAPTER 2: LOVE.....45

In Search
Love Poem
Unwanted Solitude
Love You
1 Track Mind of Us
Her Beauty
Addict
The Happiness of Her
Description
Proverbs 31 Woman
Just a Friend
This Man's Views

Realization of a Lonely One
Special #1
I Want to Be This for You
Let Me Show You

CHAPTER 3: FEARFUL.....67

Psychological Track Star
The Reason This Lonely Guy Is
0 Relationships with 2 Attempts with 1 Aggressive Girl
             And 1 Introduction
Cowardly Man
The Confession Told Too Little Too Late
Blinding Beauty
The One Who Jones for Love But Keep Themselves From It

CHAPTER 4: FAMILY.....81

Sincere AP
Prisoner's Illness
The Search Goes on
How I Felt Before My Mom Got Well
Found Revelations in Your Absence

INTRODUCTION

I was born and raised in Chicago, Illinois. I am now entering my junior year at Alabama A & M University, as a finance major. In the fifth grade I was assigned to memorize "We Wear the Mask" by Paul Laurence Dunbar, and I have been writing poetry since that time. Once I got that first glimpse of poetry I was hooked. I began looking up different poets and trying to find more and more about this craft. The more I researched, the more inspired I became to write. Although I was young, I had been going through a very stressful time. I wasn't one who had many friends in grammar school, and I tended to be closed off at home. Poetry became my release and my therapy, and it has progressed over time until now. This is my first book, and as you read, you should be able to experience me in the best way I can express myself which is through poetry--my therapy.

So, I hope you enjoy the journey you're about to embark upon through my past and present experiences: my trials and tribulations; resolutions and clarifications that I've been through, have overcome, and finally come to. I pray My Words help you as much, if not more than they have helped me.

Terrence T. Carter

November, 2008

CHAPTER 1
WORDS

PATH OF LIFE

God gave man 2 things

Freewill and many choices

From those choices the outcome of our minds, lives, and souls are determined

I pray the Lord will lead me on the path of wisdom and righteousness

I pray I make the right decisions on that path

Sometimes I find a mirror and recite this poem to myself

And find total contentment with me being my own audience

I let my eyes become the compass

To guide me to a better life

As a man

A good man

And not being an old boy

Who is mentally stuck in time

Acting as a child as an adult

So I end this poem to be continued

Because I haven't gone down this path long enough

To finish this poem

On this path I call LIFE

CONTINUING ON THE PATH

On my path of life I continue
walking down this road
Trials and tribulations make the road muddy
making it hard for me to walk
strengthening my steps
as I move on
and once the terrain clears
the mud leaves the print of my feet
letting those in my surroundings
and letting me know where I came from
and so I shall never forget

THE YESTERDAYS OF ME

I had felt defeated so long
I accepted it
and with that acceptance
I accepted all that needed to be denied
the failing
the not taking care of my responsibilities
being ignorant of the consequences
and how they affected me and others

not seeking wisdom through those mistakes
but trying to let others suffer the consequences for my actions

the procrastination
the putting off till tomorrow
when tomorrow is a gamble
because tomorrow is not promised

The man who put off till tomorrow

today died incompetent because he never
finished what he started

today blindly thinking he had tomorrow
when today was his last day

The mediocrity
the letting barely be good enough
hindering the unlocking of my true potential
keeping myself ignorant of what I'm truly capable of !

The negativity
the allowing of ridicule, bad habits,

and falsehoods of others
in my surroundings

the self-pity bringing upon self-loathing

bringing upon a deep depression within me
At this time I shut my eyes from the truth
purposely making myself ignorant of my problems

because I felt inconvenienced

in not knowing
with not knowing the need

for change is not known
yet the need is still there

But as life goes on

people grow as I did
and through growth the acceptance

of that bitter taste of defeat

slowly began fading away

with a sweet taste being victorious
I end this. . . to be continued
because I have yet to do all that is needed to be done
and this poem shall go on till it is all done
but since no more has been done

I can go no further
just reminisce on my yesterdays

so they won't happen today....

THIS IS WHY I'M ABSTINENT

Today's generation feels abstinence is to deprive oneself of
                                                         sexual pleasure
and if you're abstinent you're a minority of today's generation.

Some feel to be in the norm is the way to be, so they let themselves fall under the majority of today's youth.
But I'm one of few who know that to wait till marriage is not to deprive myself of something and my virginity is not a disease as many look at it to be.

Virginity, in actuality, is not the deprivation of sensual, sexual, erotic pleasure
Yet a divine condom or safeties station from the real disease, the S.T.Ds such as:
       *Crabs that bring upon a sensational itch in places
                                                 unmentionable
       *The big G aka gonorrhea burning so making the hardest
          of thugs plead and beg,
          scream and flee to the free clinic when they pee

I think some of you know first hand what I mean.
And that's only 2 of some hundred odd members of the V.D. family

I'll call this next group the incurables
that bring upon much pain remove them and its name is herpes
       *then there's the gruesome twosome, brother and sister
          H.I.V. and H.P.V.
These viruses kill many men and women globally everyday.

Do you still think its virginity?
       That's only one of many reasons I keep my virginity

The main reason I keep my virginity intact is because of what it truly does
which is not the depriving but the preserving of something precious and priceless

The internal, external, mental, physical, emotional
and most of all spiritual purity,
and I will keep my virginity protected, as a mother would her child,
like a precious jewel, and it will be given to
                        one and only one special woman

PROPER SECURITY

Safe sex is all good and well

The questions is which method truly prevails

Latex is the most common choice of use

Yes, it does stop the seeds' passage through

But HIV and STDs--that is another story

High percentage of efficiency

Yes

But not high enough for me

See, I have a no tolerance policy

When it comes to the security of my body

So use at your own risk

Don't get me wrong

if you do engage in sexual activity

Latex is the best instrument to use

Just make sure to critique this instrument of safe sex

And use it properly

But for me personally

My instrument is full proof

100% efficiency

What is it you ask

It is me--ABSTINENCE

Yes, the true exercise of strengthening the virtuous trait of patience
And with this subject the popular saying is "No glove, No love "
But in my case it is '"Without wed, there will be no bed"
This is a message to all old & young
If you feel you are ready for sexual activity
Use the proper security

MY WALK

It's said everything in life happens for a reason

And all the bad things are just trials and tribulations

And we are to use them as stepping stones

And we are to use these stepping stones to build upon

But I'm tired of these stairs

All these stairs

It seems I've climbed so high

I have reached beyond earth

But what am I complaining about

I know so many people who have it worse

See in actuality I have not climbed enough

Through pain and suffering comes growth and I can suffer so much more

I really should be thanking God for all I have right now

And the last thing I should be doing is complaining for what I've been through

When it has made me the man I am right now

Such a man is hard to find today

A man who loves the Lord

A man of integrity

A man who uses self control instead of birth control

A man who knows you can't put a price on love and the ones you love

A man who acts like a man and not a boy

A man who knows to take responsibility for his actions

A man who not only knows these things

But puts his knowledge to action . . .

So I'm going to stop talking the talk

And continue walking the walk

SURROUNDINGS

Serenity and tranquility

The surroundings

I thrive to be in consistently

But no matter how much I duck and dodge

Drama seems to find its way in my path

And I can't get any peace

Because I have too much bottled up inside

Cinque said, "Give us free"

I need to say, "Give me free"

No longer enslaving my soul with all these things inside of me

    Stressed out

WHEN MY EYES SEE THEMSELVES

This is what I have seen in my 16
as I looked at myself, I saw the instrument I was using
to do so, and I saw anger. I continued to look, and I looked
deep and wondered
the where, the why, the what could bring
such an anger within me.

As I continued to look,
I pondered what it is I was wondering, and I thought to myself
(I haven't gone through any thing the next person
hasn't been through, yet it's not what I've been through,
but what I've seen).
These things that I have seen,
and I continued to look and think.
As I think,
I picture the things I've seen:
the lies that have been spoken,
the wiping out of nations
by disease,
starvation,

        the corruption of young minds
   by the bringing of yesterday's irrelevance today
      so we will not look to tomorrow.

These things I see—
    the corruption--
    the starving--
    the poverty--
the difficulties of immigration
to the land of the proud and free yet this proud land is very costly.
What's the bill for 400 years of slavery,
600 years of open discrimination that has paid
every race except none wanting of change Caucasian. . .
a land so proud when in reality
it has no integrity. . .
a nation that gives a month to celebrate 4,000,000 years of accomplishments
but only recognizes the accomplishments made after slavery.

    Showing only 200 of the 4,000,000 years of history.
  My eye of anger began to weep in sorrow from this realization.
    I turned from the mirror and toward a book of knowledge.
   I saw not what be of the world but what the world could be:
     a world that is not the playground of the evil one

a world with no tree of knowledge
a world without war of the world
a world without war of races
a world without war of religions
a world where we have one nature

WHY I WRITE

Poetry . . .

Flow with me on the river banks of my creativity

On the outside I may seem cowardly

But on the inside these raging rapids of words are courageous

Showing all the things I'm afraid to

Share with any one

Nothing left unsaid

All is opened and free

All these feelings going back and forth on these

Raging rapids of my creativity

Yet you feel a sense of tranquility

And your chest is free because there's nothing to get off of it

Although I may be too cowardly to display these things with my mouth

I write them down

And I let my writings become my mouthpiece

And I find tranquility in my poetry

WRITER'S BLOCK

My way of venting has been capped

I feel like a shaken up pop bottle ready to explode

With all these emotions inside of me

It seems if I feel one more thing I'm going to implode

We as a people are own therapists

And use many things as therapeutic release

Some use basketball

Some use weightlifting

Some use many other tasks

But I use my pen and paper to let out

My past aggressions

Present passions

Future romance

My hidden feelings

But I have been blocked

My road to recovery has a roadblock

And I have yet to get my breakthrough

Because I have yet to break through this block

I fell trapped

While on the outside I seem free

But on the inside I feel confined

I am by myself with this cluttered mind
With all these un-thought about thoughts
But not un-thought thoughts
But these thought not thought through
Now I realize I didn't fully think everything through
So my mind is not cluttered but incomplete
And an incomplete mind leaves an incomplete poem
Which means I'm through

RECOVERY

But now see I can't be through
Because I feel this block releasing
And I feel me breaking through
The dam has collapsed
That was holding my words back
These words are flowing through like a raging rapid
These words that are in me are going berserk
This writer's block has become a writer's surplus
Should I be thankful for this what I call a writer block
Because it gave me a period of thinking
Because it help me with my incoherent incomplete thoughts
Telling my mind to shut up and think
Like it was a gregarious fool
Going on about everything
 This silenced me and forced me to listen
Because I was halfway ignorant and now I'm fully knowledgeable
Of self

IN THE KNOW

There are to many of us who are not in the know

Carter G. Woodson said it best "When you control a man's thinking, you don't have to worry about his actions"

Because knowledge is power

And once you begin to think you shall know

And to know is a powerful thing

And to gain this power you must use intelligence, you see

Which is commonly mistaken as being smart

When in actuality it is the ability to think and learn

Which we all have but few use

Because many of us abuse the opportunities we have

One in particular is our advancement in education

Which is the acquiring of knowledge

And from the saying this is the acquiring of power

But we miss-use the key time to do so

And choose the opportune time for gaining mass

Consumption of power to play instead

Not using your intelligence to realize this is utter ignorance

Which is a lack of knowledge

Showing weakness

Because once again I say "knowledge is power"

And to be ignorant is a lack thereof
And not to know is the only sane reason I can think of
that we would not take full advantage
to learn as much as possible
And you would have to be crazy to know this and ignore it
Because as men we're in a constant pursuit of strength
which is a synonym of power
And the one with the most power is dominant
And through this if you don't see the importance of education
And continue to repeat the same mistakes
you are guilty of the act of stupidity
So I beg you to take heed to this message
And get in the know

AROUND YOU WHEN IT'S CONVENIENT

Phases

These phases I go through

It seem as if every other minute I'm feeling something different

And it has me going through mazes emotionally

Constantly having ups and downs

When it seems I'm moving forward, something turns me right back around

I want to be happy, but my face seems to be stuck in a frown

And lately it seems I'm only down

No one to turn to while in unwanted solitude

I turn to the friend of the friendless

It's funny how we can run when we're in need

But when called upon we seem a bit sluggish

At least I do

See I know I'm a bit selfish

Only going to the Lord when it's convenient for me

After I'm uplifted and delivered from my grief

When I feel there's no more need

I flee

From the one who helped me

No longer in the Word

So my conscience is whispering

I can't really hear it clearly

Whereas before, there was an uproar of conviction

Screaming no more

Before it began

Keeping me out of many situations

Saving my life more than likely

Because those situation could have had me dead in the end

And I can't understand how I could constantly neglect the Lord

I'm going to use these words as a humility poem

Humbling me when I feel I'm no longer in need

And remind me whom to stay close to

PERCEPTION

It is said that black is beautiful
And the saying is true
But many of us as black people don't see that
You glue your eyes shut to the beauty that is you
It is time to see
What is me
What are you
What are we
Black

B. L. A. C. K
B eautiful
L ooking for knowledge continuously
A ction taken to improve self
C ommunicating with all
K nowing knowledge is meant to be share
And not kept to oneself making it useless
Yet America shows Black as
B lack on black crime
L ack of education
A cting a fool

C laiming welfare checks

K illing ourselves

Who's to blame

Both

But it is up to us as blacks to eliminate one

Which one is up to us

Perception

CARPE DIEM

If time is of the essence
Then I am essence-less
I don't even know what this means
See, that's what happens
When you waste time you become ignorant
Constantly procrastinating
See, people only count on me to put off till next
Each time
I'm pretty much the opposite of carpe diem
I barely see the day--let alone seize the day
Blindly searching for where the day went
And it seems time is faster than me
Because it keeps passing me by
Why
I don't know I'll find out tomorrow
But little did I know
Death has its appointment with me tomorrow
So I don't have tomorrow; I only have today
And I say time must be faster than I
Time must be faster than me because it keeps passing me by
Just as life has

We don't know how much time we have

So I say carpe diem people carpe diem

To seize the day because

Everyday is precious--every moment is sacred

And every second should be spent doing what you love and improving self

POEM FOR TIMYRA

I had lost my destiny

I looked left

I looked right

I looked behind me

Screaming to myself

Destiny where are you? Destiny where are you?

Then there's destiny starring me right in the face saying

Open you eyes and you'll see me

Or just turn towards me

And stop seeking for what's not lost

Because it costs time and that's non-refundable

Then you don't listen

Because you spend more time trying to get back the time you already spent

Destiny saying how many times do I have to tell you

The clock of life is doing what you should be doing

Constant forward movement

But you keep back pedaling looking at the

Past (back then) letting your

Present (right now) pass you by disrupting your

Future (what could be)

When what you should be doing instead is looking forward

So you will look towards me

And see what destiny has in store for you

Now what is destiny you say?

Honestly I don't know the Webster's dictionary meaning per say

But in my eyes destiny is our pre-determined purpose that lies before us

And from the meaning and dealing with myself personally

I have looked back far too many times,

Hindering me of finding my true purpose

Looking back at my past mistakes instead of learning from them

Trying to erase them and in doing so trying to get back time that has already been spent

In doing that making another mistake

Not seeking my past mistakes as present warnings so they won't happen again

But I keep running into them

Because I don't see them

Constantly looking back

Tracking down these same mistakes that keep trapping me

Yes, I am guilty

Because that was me

But I now look forward seeing what my purpose has for me

And now that you know me

Ask yourself am I looking forward

Or dwelling in the past?

THE INCOHERENT THINKING'S OF ME

Simplicity is not for me

Complexity seems to be in my destiny

The thing is I take nothing lightly

I make everything difficult in my pathway

These are the words of one who feels sorry for oneself

Feels as if the world is against him

So he can't trust anyone

So my guard must be up at all times

I lash out when you confront my wrongs

But quick to tell you your crimes

I allow no one on my side

I have to look over my shoulder at all times

But it's cool

I'll just be that loner type

Don't need nobody's going to get what I need

The most honest way I can get it

Yes, this is an unnecessary struggle

My pride allows me to do this repeatedly

Making me guilty of the crime of stupidity

I know this because I hear the sirens in my head

The police need to lock me up and throw away the key

So I can realize the errors of me

I must change my ways because I don't want to die lonely

So stuck in my ways can't even turn to my family

Living in a house where we're supposed to be loved ones

But I turned them into strangers

In my mind the only thing holding us together was a last name

Pretty much pigeonholing them with a person in the street

With the last name Carter or Williams

The saying "Blood is thicker than water" I laugh at it

I'm beginning to grasp it

But I'm starting to think it's too late

And the only one who can exodus me from this solitary paranoia is Moses with the help of God

Forget that—That's' my old ways coming back

Finding comfort in my misery

Or the fear of using it to run from my problems

I do it so much you could call me a track star

Through writing this poem

I'm going to chain cinderblocks to my feet and throw away the key

So I'm forced to stand still and face the trials before me

And there will be nothing but growth and a gaining of maturity in me

With all this needless pleading that took me to a higher state of mind

And the cinderblocks that I thought would help me

Were in actuality holding me back from forward movement

So I released myself in agreement with myself

No longer to hold myself back

And to leave this place of negativity

Allow myself to grasp my true potential

Like a wave of creativity that will overtake me

And the only one who can free me from this self-made bondage is GOD

WORDS

words
oh these words
what they do
words that give a feeling of warm affection
yet they give a feeling of a bottomless pit of sorrow
what they do
words I have said, didn't say, could have, maybe even should have said.
what they do
words are said to not hurt, but sticks and stones can
yet these words can feel like logs and boulders.
words so irritating that they make me wish for silence
yet words that are filled with wisdom and so profound that I desire to hear sermons of them.
words give me feelings that are diverse.
what words do to me I've just said
what do words do to you?
words can only tell

CHAPTER 2
LOVE

IN SEARCH

I'm in search for the one for me
Therefore, I shall maintain my purity
But our purity shall entwine together
And we shall become one
Because you shall be my happiness
And I am yours
You and I are a two-piece puzzle
And we complete each other

LOVE POEM

LOVE is new to me
Chrisette Michele said, "It's you"
the question is
Who?
or better yet is it true?
I have felt this for very few
as I recall it has only been you
heart throbbing
all other thoughts subsiding
leaving me to think of only you
I say again this is new
so if I'm saying it wrong
I am deeply apologetic
I would say it right if I only knew
well it's no mystery
you need no clue
it is quite relevant that I love you
and there should be no question
who
because love is the who
see this is my love letter to LOVE

so I assumed if you love LOVE

LOVE would love you back

foolishly assuming

making a fool out of myself

I found out

LOVE doesn't work like that

as a matter of fact

LOVE only loves LOVE back

and puts together those who love each other

so where does that leave me

still waiting patiently for that package from LOVE

from the one that loves me

UNWANTED SOLITUDE

I am tired of being alone.
I am tired of this feeling of incompleteness
I am tired of being happy,
but sad at the same time because
there is no one to share my happiness with.
I am tired of being sad and becoming sadder
because there is no one there to comfort me.
maybe that's why I am so quick to comfort others.
this is my plea for a companion
      my Eve
      my rib
I am rib-less Adam
I am man without his woman
I am boy without his girl
I am looking for the apple of my eye.
      in continuous search
I am in UNWANTED SOLITUDE

LOVE YOU

I'm not a confrontational person

But when it comes to you

I'm willing to confront all obstacles that try to bring distance between us

I do this because you're special

You're no ordinary woman

That why I'm willing to do extraordinary things for you

See, as a man I'm sight-oriented

But I am drawn to more than your looks

I want to know what's on your mind

What you think, as you are mine

And I thank GOD for blessing me with you

Because the time I spend with you is miraculous

Yes, we have our ups and downs

But I'm willing to try to keep the downs from outweighing the ups

And keep your frown turned upside down

I do this because you embody true beauty

And I would go on to tell you how beautiful you are

But that would downgrade you by trying to describe your beauty

that has obviously surpassed words

So I'll end this by letting you know

I LOVE YOU

1 TRACK MIND OF US

In her flaws
I don't want to chastise or bring her down
    but to inform her
In a way where I still put a smile on her face
To the point where she finds happiness in
Bettering herself by herself
    and through my help
The way I see it
If we have a difference
It is not a problem but a possibility
To grow closer and know more about one another
    day by day
Becoming more and more intelligent of the fact that
We are the two-piece puzzle
    that completes each other
I never thought I would find someone who fits me
It's mind boggling to me
That we have so much in common
And at the same time so different
    and somehow it works
In time understanding will come

So confused at these happenings
Because for so long I felt like one
Who was destined to be in eternal solitude
    to have no one
But to be blessed with such a blessing
    is truly miraculous
To have someone wanting companionship
    as much as I want it
I may focus on other things
Yet I always find myself
    coming back to You and me
Because I don't know
    how I went from that to this

HER BEAUTY

This is you in my eyes
Your beauty is divinity personified
This means your beauty is heavenly
To have heavenly beauty is to be
Beautiful inside and out
Your beauty is angelic
When I see you
I'm overwhelmed by a sense of tranquility
It is as if the Lord were to make sweet music
And you are the masterpiece
That was the outcome
You're like a smooth melodic melody
And when I see you, the feeling is indescribable
And I thank God
Because it is a blessing to have seen
Her beauty which is your beauty

ADDICT

For all couples

I do no drugs
So I let you become my intoxication
I have become addicted to you
I am an addict for you

THE HAPPINESS OF HER

Your laughter is like the laughter of a newborn child
      Adorable
On my darkest day to call in desperation of comfort.
      To hear your voice have happiness in it
      brightens my day at the speed of thought
So I selfishly say, "Stay happy,"
      and I shall live to make you smile

DESCRIPTION

As beautiful as a lotus blossom in the spring
As strong as bamboo

Wise as a redwood
Self-sustaining as a grape vine
Who am I?
A beautiful in & out woman

PROVERBS 31 WOMAN

My Proverbs 31 Woman
A woman who knows I can't sing
But if she wants to hear it anyway
It'll be like I just wanna sing Musiq's 143
    Because I love you
        To the point where I want to make a covenant
            Between us 3
                You
                Me
                &
                GOD
See, if I was to go blind at this very second
Standing in front of you
I wouldn't wallow in grief
Because my last sight was well spent
Seeing the embodiment of true beauty
That is you
My Proverbs 31 Woman
What are you but priceless
My past work shows I am a shy guy
But I can't help but be open and display my feelings to you

Because when I saw you the wall that was fear
Became all but a stepping stone
That I stepped over to get to you
See, my Proverbs 31 Woman
Makes me do things I once felt to be impossible
Yeah, my Proverbs 31 Woman
And that's all I know about her
        until I find out her name
        And find her
Yeah, my Proverbs 31 Woman
Hope to see you soon

JUST A FRIEND

She sees me as just a friend
She sees me as just a friend
O Baby, I'm always there when you're in need
But she sees me as just a friend
Because she said
I never showed her I could be there for her in that way
Well, this is me being sick & tired of being sick & tired
Of being lonely because of the fear of no one wanting me
        No more
I'm going for mine
Looking for a relationship where her happiness is my happiness
It just so happens I shall be the root of her happiness
So now I'm in the pursuit of happiness

THIS MAN'S VIEWS

a woman who doesn't contradict herself
    saying she wants a good guy
        but instead of that she goes to the gangsta trash
a woman who takes me for me
a woman who makes me be better
    and wants me to better myself to insure her happiness
a woman who doesn't punish me for the discouragement
    brought on by another
a woman who accepts the fact that all I want is to help mend the wounds
      and not open old ones or make new ones

REALIZATION OF A LONELY ONE

Nobody knows the grief in me
Nobody knows the misery I feel
Loneliness seems to be eternally destined for me
Where is that lady for me?
But I guess I'm being a bit overzealous since I'm only 18
But being in love with being in love
Makes it difficult to wait patiently
But I haven't truly waited
Because I've searched unthinkingly
Because 'm looking where it seems not to exist
      and all just like and mistake infatuation for love
It's said you don't appreciate what you have until it's gone
So am I divinely appreciative of this
Because I've obviously yet to experience
      this mental, emotional, physical,
      and most of all spiritual intimacy
         I so long for
Like an orphan for the love of his birth mother
Maybe it's not a divinity-personified appreciation
But I think the saying is wrong
      Or not so much wrong as it is incomplete

Yes, it's true when something is lost, it is truly appreciated
But when something is seen so much and not experienced,
    it is appreciated beyond means to say what you mean
So to all who hear this, pray
Because if you're going through what I'm going through,
    you can only rely on God to truly guide you
And please pray for me because I'm praying for you
Because those of us who put ourselves
    in this land of loneliness need it
And I thank you, Lord, for giving me these words,
    for helping this lonely one to stop searching for
        what is not meant to be found but shall come to me
            when it is supposed to,
        if it is supposed to
    With saying this I am gaining the virtue of patience
Waiting for love to make its appointment with me

SPECIAL # 1

From the first time I saw your face
I knew there was none who could replace this feeling
    This feeling of fulfillment
    This feeling of completeness
It was as if my life was a puzzle
    And you were that missing peace
It was as if you were the rib
    that was taken to make woman
    And I was your Adam, and you were my Eve
You are that special one
That one that I have been looking for
That one for me
That one I could say those 3 words to
    And it would be genuine
You are the one for me
    And I love you

I WANT TO BE THIS FOR YOU

This is how I feel
This is what I want you to do for me
And what I want to be for you
Touch me, tease me
Kiss and adore me
Love me
Only put one before me
And that's GOD
Because all I want to do is love and cherish you
And I would only put one before you
And that is the one you put before me
Because I just want to be your friend
I want to be your man
Accept me for who I am
Don't try to change me
Keep me as I am
And only help to improve me
As I will you
Because we all have our flaws
And I don't want you to be afraid to show them to me
Please just choose me

Don't reject me

Because I just want to be your advisor

I want to be your confidant

For you to be able to come to me

    When in need of advice

        Or just to get something off your chest

So once again just choose me

And don't misuse me

Take my love and cherish it as I would yours

Because I just want to be your comforter

I want to be that shoulder you can lean on

I don't want you to be afraid to show me your pain

I'm not here to exploit or exceed it

But to ease it

I won't abuse or misuse you

Just cherish you as much as I can

So just take these words in consideration

And accept this admiration

Because I adore you

And don't let these words

Go in one ear and out the other

And go to another boy

Who just uses the phrase

      I love you

          As A leg spreader

Because before you is man who takes it seriously

Because I just want to be your protector

For you to come to me in your time of fear

And let me put you at ease

All in all I want to be your everything and you mine

LET ME SHOW YOU

I want to write a love poem

A lover's poem so sincere that you can't help but love me

And as much as I would want to write this poem

It's not possible

Because no combination of words can express this in its purest sincerity

Only through action this can be displayed

So I can only show you through my deeds

All I ask is for you to let me show you

CHAPTER 3
FEARFUL

PSYCHOLOGICAL TRACK STAR

The lack of confronting the obstacles that lay before me
Because of my fear of confrontation
Turns me psychologically into a track star
Because I am constantly in pursuit of
The opposite direction
That I need to be confronting

THE REASON THIS LONELY GUY IS ↓

I know I may seem down a lot

Just lonely

I used to say it was because I was bringing it on myself

Because I feared approaching young women who intrigued me with the possibility of rejection

Then I amped myself up

Saying I'm a good guy

Clean, respectful, goal-oriented, somewhat romantic,

And sensitive to a certain extent

Yeah, I'm a good guy

So I begin approaching

Only to get what I feared

    Rejected

These many rejections from all types of women

 Have led to this conclusion

I'm looking for the one but he is in the mirror

I'm my one

Destined to spend my days solitary

So if you wonder why I'm down

Because I'm coping with the reality

That my other is non-existent

And I shall have a heart full of love that wants to be
Given intimately but shall not be given to the one who
Shall give back the same type of love

0 RELATIONSHIPS
2 ATTEMPTS WITH
1 AGGRESSIVE GIRL
AND 1 INTRODUCTION

My Junior year in math class

She sat by me

She asked for help with a problem

After the equation was solved

And class ended

We went to lunch

I got to know her

She got to know me

We got to know each other

But we didn't get together

This has happened time & time again

Why you say

I say I fear rejection

But it's a lie

Because I truly fear approaching her

Because I'm unbearably shy

My shyness is like bitterness

But instead of anger my appreciation grows

And not letting it out is destroying me

Just to say those three words would put me at ease

For me just to say to her "I --- like you"

You begin to like them so much

It makes you do things. . .

Like, like, like, "Have you ever liked someone so much

Your happiness didn't matter to you

Because her happiness is your happiness?

And when she has a tear on her face

You have 1000 inside

But you don't show it to better comfort her

And you keep your shoulder dry and open for her tear

Yes, it hurts you to see her with the one who hurts her

But because of my fear of approaching her

I continue to give advice to prolong her happiness

Even though it prolongs my sorrow

Even though she is happy

I am miserable

Because I am not her other

This continues until time moves on without you

She moves on as well

And we grow distant until I'm nothing but a vague memory to her

And the solution to this is I don't know

Because I still suffer from the shyness that's keeping me from the one for me

That's why I have had

    0 relationships

    2 attempts with

    1 aggressive girl

    And 1 introduction

COWARDLY MAN

You are beautiful in every way
And I want to be with you
But this isn't even said to you
This is me daydreaming about you
And what I would say
If I wasn't a coward
So until the day
I just bring it upon myself to have the courage
This is how I shall feel and you shall never know
As long as I am a cowardly man
Because although I want to be your man
Being a cowardly man
Is keeping me from doing so

THE CONFESSION TOLD TOO LITTLE TOO LATE

I once heard

"I slept in my uniform last night because I wanted to win today"

This statement intrigued me and I felt in a way I could relate:

When I sleep with my book in hand, I'm ready to learn tomorrow

When I sleep with my Bible in hand, I'm ready for the understanding of future situations

When I sleep with you in my heart and mind

    My love for you is always

I know you have a man

and the feelings you have for him I cannot change

But the feelings I have for you are eternal

I've tried to ignore these feelings but they won't go away

If it is a sin to feel this way

This is a sin I'm willing to bare

The love I have for you

Is a love I can't live without

It is as if it is my air

By saying this

I end this conversation in despair

Because your Other is not I

And I cannot bear to tell you this

Because you are no longer there

BLINDING BEAUTY

Your beauty is blinding

Because you're radiantly bright

Yes, I know these two things mean the same thing

But you're so beautiful I had to say it twice

Your beauty is intoxicating

I can't get enough of looking at you

I know what you're thinking

That I'm attracted to only what I see physically

I not only use my eyes to see you

I use my ears to hear your beautiful intellect

And your beautiful voice

So when I say

I can't get enough of looking at you

I mean I love listening to you

Don't get me wrong your physical beauty is appealing to me as well

But that's only one part of you

There's so much more to you than the eye can see

That's why I used all of me to see all of you

In doing so, I know your beauty is through and through

So I say once again

When I say

I can't get enough of looking

You know now I'm not only using the sight of eye

But my mind and spirit

And this lets me know your beauty is true

Although we have had many conversations

I have never told you

Yes, I know I am a fool

I know I am a fool!

Because the beauty displayed by you

Should be told to you daily because it is true

But I let my arch nemesis Fear keep me from telling you

So I just look at the blinding beauty that is you

And allow myself to be pleasantly blinded by you.

THE ONE WHO JONESES FOR LOVE AND KEEPS THEMSELVES FROM IT

Love Jones

I'm Jonesing for love

But I have no one to love me

Which puts me in a bit of a predicament

Because I have a lot of love to give

With no one to give it to

I feel like a child who ran to the candy store just to find out it was closed

But in my case I'm the one who is locking the door

Keeping myself from the possibility of finding the one who loves me

And the one I should love

It is said if you ask not, you have not

It is true

I have not asked so don't have right now

I have not even asked her name

And I do not have any knowledge of her

Just a mental picture

that appears every time I close my eyes

The faces continue to change

because I let fear get in the way of my opportunity

To find the one who can fill this empty spot in my side

I'm constantly saying the words

Because the words are easy to say

The actions are where the challenge lies

Putting myself out there in state of vulnerability of what a I dread

It starts with an "R" and can be summed up in a two-letter word

It's amazing how much power I allow this word to have over me

When I think about it

It's pretty absurd to let the fear of one word alter my actions

Forcefully forgetting my attractions that I have

Toward those whom I would like to approach

So I use this as a message to stop being a punk

What's the worst that can happen?

All she can say is "No"

CHAPTER 4
FAMILY

SINCERE AP

I said I'm sorry for what was done

But I guess it was wasn't sincere

Because I'm being destroyed by the bitterness in me

Although I hide with a smile, a joke, or laughter
When in reality I'm continuously in sorrow

Crying on the inside because I've cried so much my tears have become dry

And I programmed myself to make my tears to go in reverse

So I can only cry on the inside

Some days it's easy to hide--some days it's not
It's like a cancer rapidly killing me mentally

It would be easier to be true if you didn't give so many empty promises
If you'd talked to me and not at me
But I'm not occupied to judge
Just to forgive and ask for forgiveness
It's just so hard to forget
But I will stop trying to forget so I can look out for the same thing

that's been happening since I was 7

a continuous cycle that has been going on

Yet I will dig deep in the black hole that I have formed with the bitterness

that has tried to consume my soul

And I apologize for the lack of communication, therefore, hiding my feelings,

    excluding one, like the older brother of the prodigal son

And I forgive you for missed birthdays, your days, graduations and communication

With saying this a ton has been lifted
Unfortunately it hasn't been said so I maintain

    with the weight of this unnecessary bitterness

    living life on the edge because tomorrow is promised to one

    and that one isn't me

So I'm endanger of dying with regret and without the reconciliation of my

    FIRST TEACHERS

Let go of all bitterness you have towards those in your life

It only brings about self-destruction

PRISONER'S ILLNESS

Mother, where art thou?

Your children are in need of you

But you can't hear us pleading

Because you keep going in & out

Of these steeled bared door like they're revolving doors

When will it be time to say "No more"?

And for you to give up these deviant ways

When will you understand that

Fast cash leads to no cash

And all you can get is commissary

You said you do it because you didn't want to ask for money any more

But when you get caught and then while incarcerated you constantly beg and plead

With those to whom you refused to display your need

What is the sense in that with me saying this

Once you get out I don't want you to turn back to ways of old

A constant cycle, going around and round

I call it prisoner's illness

Which means you feel the need to do the same old stuff

Which puts you right back in

Why are we addicted to our past sins?

We can't say we're not because we do them over and over again
And when someone confronts you on it
You act like nothing is wrong
Then you begin to defend what you are doing wrong
You're set in your ways
You think what you're doing wrong is right
In actuality you're blind
And I'm determined to show you the light
And the right path
I will never give up on you
I will show you as many times as I need to
For you to change
Yeah I may sound like broken record
Saying the same thing over and over again
But it seems like I have to because you never listen
Because you put yourself in the same predicament
Doing the same old thing
Showing symptoms of prisoner's illness
Lord willing, in the process of your incarceration
You will consume the knowledge needed
And see the error of your ways
And get out of these phases
I know it's said that bad habits die hard

And I plan to use this poem as a vaccine to this ongoing illness
And when I read it to you, I let loose on those habits
And slowly but surely a change shall come
And you shall no longer suffer from prisoner's illness

THE SEARCH GOES ON

Written August 8, 2005

This is not about a girl
but a woman   a mother   a mother with an addiction   an addiction that took her away
      with her gone the system came in and left but left with
                              my siblings

Who's to blame?

    is it a negligent brother with harbored feelings toward his mother for abandonment
      for loving a drug more than her child?

is it an addicted mother with only the pursuit to get that next fix?

I feel that both had a part
    the brother for not trying harder to resolve the situation
    the mother for making the situation

and the consequence is today

    3 years 9 months 18 days
    since I last saw Tamara who was growing & learning so fast
      she was 3 last time I saw her

    Tyron so small, so innocent it was as if I looked at my baby
                    picture when I looked at him
    when I saw him he was 3 months last time I saw him

Yet the search goes on for the reuniting of my family

    for the restoration of the relationship between a brother
                    and his younger siblings
    between a mother and the rehabilitation of her purity,
               sanity, and salvation

      the day this search ends is the day of my great throne
                                              judgment

      until then

The Search Goes on. . .

Sometime later I found myself at a time where I grew weary and felt like giving up in my search

But then the Lord blessed me with finding a brother I didn't know existed on July 16, 2006

      I got to hear his voice on July 21, 2006
      I got to see his face August 6, 2006

Although I felt weary then, I am weary no more

I am energized and The Search Goes on. . .

LOST NOW FOUND

What was once lost has been found
The reuniting of a brother and his younger siblings
Continuously building our relationship
In pursuit to grow so close and create bond so tight
That we shall never part again

The regaining of a mother's sanity though throwing away her drug
    addiction
In doing so now in current pursuit of permanent sobriety
Realizing she could not lose her salvation
So she put her trust in the Lord and
Fully surrendered her burden to Him
And He is bringing her through
And I am thanking God continuously for making
A way out of no way
For showing grace to this young man who was a boy
Who lost his siblings and his mother
But through Him who is greater
What was lost is now found

HOW I FELT BEFORE MY MOM GOT WELL

I was killing myself by keeping my feelings on the inside.
Writing this poem helped to let them out.

I have not seen my mother in a while
But I have these dreams where she comes back.
When she comes back, it feels as if I'm in a fairy tale.
It's like there can be no wrong.
It's as if God made us perfect.
And all I lost I found.
The sun rose over the empty sky
And transformed a forever-lasting cold night into a warm bright day.
An emotional tidal wave wiped out all hate,
Breaking down the barriers of insecurity
To bring out the harbored bitterness stored deep inside,
Releasing all feelings until there was nothing left
But understanding and love.
All this happened the day she came back.

Then I woke from my dream to my nightmare,
And I realized what I felt was like a fairy tale was just that, a tale.
When I awoke, I could find no right, but wrong was all around.
When I awoke, I was no longer in God's world of perfection,
Yet I found myself in the devil's world of corruption.
When I awoke, there was no sun to bring day,
Just cold darkness in the sky of the everlasting night.
When I awoke, there were many unspoken words, bottled up feelings,
And bitterness stored deep in the middle of my soul.

Even when I was awake she came back, but she didn't stay
And every time I waited for her when she left.
When she did come back I pleaded with
her to take care of my brother and sister.
I let her know we needed her guidance, wisdom, love, and compassion.
I would weep every time she leaves, but it seemed she showed no sympathy
Toward these needs or me because she yet kept leaving.

I get angry so angry I feel my mother is some what of a black widow,
because of the sorrow she caused me and my sister and brother.
I would sometimes call her Queen of Black Widows.
She earns this title by loving and caring for you where you can't live without her.
When I sleep I have dreams about her.
Then she leaves and you can't stop thinking about her.
It overwhelms me so much I can't breathe without her.
It feels as if you die inside slowly leaving nothing but sorrow
So all I can do is cry.

I would go on but there's nothing else to tell,

So I wait till she comes back if she has not died.
I hope she took my advice and gave her life to God so she won't go to hell.
This is how I felt before my mom got well.

FOUND REVELATIONS IN YOUR ABSENCE

You were there to give me advice when needed
When in times of sorrow you found your way to me
so I could have someone to lean on
and your shoulder open for my tears
You told me what I needed to hear
When what I felt was good to me wasn't good for me
You kept me company when I was in unwanted solitude
No, you didn't do these things all the time
No one could
If you could, you would have achieved perfection
Which no one has
So no one could
But I focused on what was not being done,
Yet I focused too much on what was not being done
Therefore, I overlooked the things that you did for me
At the time these things seem to be micro
Now that you are no longer here, they are macro
How I wish I had realized this when you were here
Now I realized what I had
And wish it was still what I have

It's too bad it took your absence for me to truly appreciate you
Now realizing this true saying
You don't know what you have until it it's gone,
Showing me to be hard headed
Because I heard this time and time again
Yet I neglected to take heed to the warnings
Making it so that experience was the only way
for me catch wind of this reality,
That I pushed away someone special,
Not knowing how special they were until they were gone
Because of my lack of appreciation and neglect

ENDORSEMENT

Words are powerful. In the hand of the skillful poet words become a creative means of expression that often provides a striking self-portrait. Plutarch noted, "In the words are seen the state of mind and character and disposition of the speaker." In his first published collection of poetry, My Words, Terrence Carter invites you to journey with him and to discover who he is, as he shares some of his views on life and love and relates some of his past and present experiences, both the joyful and painful.

In "Why I Write Poetry" Terrence explains his passion to write and offers this invitation:

> . . . Flow with me on the river of my creativity
>
> . . . .
>
> All is opened and free
>
> All these feelings going back and forth on these
>
> Raging rapids of my creativity
>
> Yet you feel a sense of tranquility . . . .
>
> And I let my writings become my mouthpiece
>
> And I find tranquility in my poetry

Indeed, there is a quiet strength in My Words, bringing to mind a statement made by W. Gladden : "Gentle words, quiet words, are after all the most powerful words. They are more convincing, more compelling, more prevailing."

Terrence openly discusses some of the challenges he faces as he endeavors to live out his faith,

> As a man who loves the Lord,

A man of integrity . . .

A man who not only knows . . .

But puts his knowledge into actions.

He acknowledges "Such a man is hard to find today."

The ancient Chinese proverb reminds us: "If you wish to know the mind of a man, listen to his words." Terrence Carter invites you to read My Words and be enlightened.

He invites you to listen and hear his voice; listen with your heart. As you read, consider:

    words

    oh these words

    what they do

    . . . .

    words give me feelings that are diverse

    what words do to me I've just said

    what do words do to you?

    words can only tell

Lonnell E. Johnson, Ph.D.
Professor Emeritus
Otterbein College
Westerville, Ohio

www.ingramcontent.com/pod-product-compliance
Lightning Source LLC
Chambersburg PA
CBHW071832290426
44109CB00017B/1805